MY KINDERGARTEN YEAR

DAILY KEEPSAKE JOURNAL

Jennifer L. Gee
TimberBelle Press

ALL ABOUT ME IN KINDERGARTEN

NAME: _____

YEAR: 20___ - 20___   AGE: _____

SCHOOL: _____

TEACHER: _____

SOME OF MY FAVORITE THINGS

BEST FRIEND: _____

FAVORITE COLOR: _____

FAVORITE FOOD: _____

FAVORITE SUBJECT: _____

FAVORITE MOVIE: _____

FAVORITE ACTIVITY: _____

FAVORITE TOY: _____

THIS IS HOW I WRITE MY NAME

PHOTO OF ME ON FIRST DAY OF KINDERGARTEN

THIS YEAR I HOPE TO LEARN:

_____

TODAY I AM FEELING:

DAY 1

DATE: _____

TODAY I LEARNED

TODAY'S MOOD

HOMEWORK

BEST CLASS
_____

LUNCH

TOP 3 THINGS THAT HAPPENED

1

2

3

DAILY DOODLE

DAY 2

DATE: _____

TODAY I LEARNED

TODAY'S MOOD

HOMEWORK

BEST CLASS

_____

LUNCH

TOP 3 THINGS THAT HAPPENED

1

2

3

DAILY DOODLE

DAY 3

DATE: _____

TODAY I LEARNED

TODAY'S MOOD

HOMEWORK

BEST CLASS
_____

LUNCH

TOP 3 THINGS THAT HAPPENED

1

2

3

DAILY DOODLE

DAY 4

DATE: _____

TODAY I LEARNED

TODAY'S MOOD

HOMEWORK

BEST CLASS
_____

LUNCH

TOP 3 THINGS THAT HAPPENED

1

2

3

DAILY DOODLE

DAY 5

DATE: _____

TODAY'S MOOD

TODAY I LEARNED

HOMEWORK

BEST CLASS
_____

LUNCH

TOP 3 THINGS THAT HAPPENED

1

2

3

DAILY DOODLE

DAY 6

DATE: _____

TODAY I LEARNED

TODAY'S MOOD

HOMEWORK

BEST CLASS

LUNCH

TOP 3 THINGS THAT HAPPENED

1

2

3

DAILY DOODLE

DAY 7

DATE: _____

TODAY I LEARNED

TODAY'S MOOD

HOMEWORK

BEST CLASS

_____

LUNCH

TOP 3 THINGS THAT HAPPENED

1

2

3

DAILY DOODLE

DAY 8

DATE: _____

TODAY I LEARNED

TODAY'S MOOD

HOMEWORK

BEST CLASS

_____

LUNCH

TOP 3 THINGS THAT HAPPENED

1

2

3

DAILY DOODLE

DAY 9

DATE: _____

TODAY I LEARNED

TODAY'S MOOD

HOMEWORK

BEST CLASS
_____

LUNCH

TOP 3 THINGS THAT HAPPENED

1

2

3

DAILY DOODLE

DAY 10

DATE: _____

TODAY'S MOOD

TODAY I LEARNED

HOMEWORK

BEST CLASS
_____

LUNCH

TOP 3 THINGS THAT HAPPENED

1

2

3

DAILY DOODLE

DAY 11

DATE: _____

TODAY'S MOOD

TODAY I LEARNED

HOMEWORK

BEST CLASS
_____

LUNCH

TOP 3 THINGS THAT HAPPENED

1

2

3

DAILY DOODLE

DAY 12

DATE: _____

TODAY'S MOOD

TODAY I LEARNED

HOMEWORK

BEST CLASS

_____

LUNCH

TOP 3 THINGS THAT HAPPENED

1

2

3

DAILY DOODLE

DAY 13

DATE: _____

TODAY I LEARNED

TODAY'S MOOD

HOMEWORK

BEST CLASS

_____

LUNCH

TOP 3 THINGS THAT HAPPENED

1

2

3

DAILY DOODLE

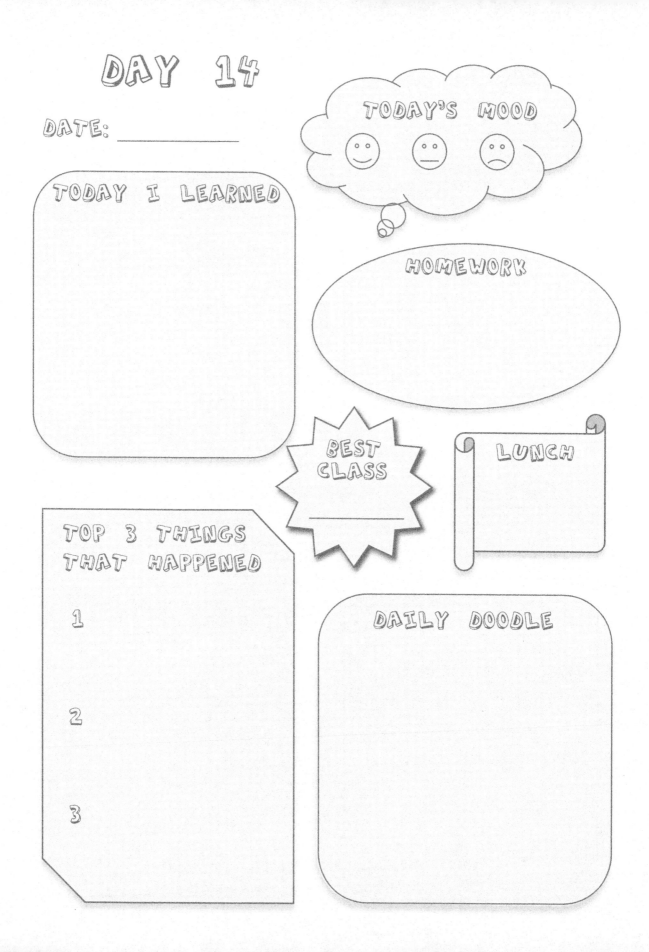

DAY 15

DATE: _____

TODAY'S MOOD

TODAY I LEARNED

HOMEWORK

BEST CLASS
_____

LUNCH

TOP 3 THINGS THAT HAPPENED

1

2

3

DAILY DOODLE

DAY 16

DATE: _____

TODAY I LEARNED

TODAY'S MOOD

HOMEWORK

BEST CLASS

LUNCH

TOP 3 THINGS THAT HAPPENED

1

2

3

DAILY DOODLE

DAY 18

DATE: _____

TODAY I LEARNED

TODAY'S MOOD

HOMEWORK

BEST CLASS
_____

LUNCH

TOP 3 THINGS THAT HAPPENED

1

2

3

DAILY DOODLE

DAY 19

DATE: _____

TODAY I LEARNED

TODAY'S MOOD

HOMEWORK

BEST CLASS

LUNCH

TOP 3 THINGS THAT HAPPENED

1

2

3

DAILY DOODLE

DAY 20

DATE: _____

TODAY I LEARNED

TODAY'S MOOD

HOMEWORK

BEST CLASS
_____

LUNCH

TOP 3 THINGS THAT HAPPENED

1

2

3

DAILY DOODLE

DAY 21

DATE: _____

TODAY I LEARNED

TODAY'S MOOD

HOMEWORK

BEST CLASS

LUNCH

TOP 3 THINGS THAT HAPPENED

1

2

3

DAILY DOODLE

DAY 22

DATE: _____

TODAY I LEARNED

TODAY'S MOOD

HOMEWORK

BEST CLASS
_____

LUNCH

TOP 3 THINGS THAT HAPPENED

1

2

3

DAILY DOODLE

DAY 23

DATE: _____

TODAY I LEARNED

TODAY'S MOOD

HOMEWORK

TOP 3 THINGS THAT HAPPENED

1

2

3

BEST CLASS

LUNCH

DAILY DOODLE

DAY 24

DATE: _____

TODAY'S MOOD

TODAY I LEARNED

HOMEWORK

BEST CLASS
_____

LUNCH

TOP 3 THINGS THAT HAPPENED

1

2

3

DAILY DOODLE

DAY 25

DATE: _____

TODAY'S MOOD

TODAY I LEARNED

HOMEWORK

BEST CLASS
_____

LUNCH

TOP 3 THINGS THAT HAPPENED

1

2

3

DAILY DOODLE

DAY 26

DATE: _____

TODAY I LEARNED

TODAY'S MOOD

HOMEWORK

BEST CLASS
_____

LUNCH

TOP 3 THINGS THAT HAPPENED

1

2

3

DAILY DOODLE

DAY 27

DATE: _____

TODAY'S MOOD

TODAY I LEARNED

HOMEWORK

BEST CLASS

LUNCH

TOP 3 THINGS THAT HAPPENED

1

2

3

DAILY DOODLE

DAY 28

DATE: _____

TODAY I LEARNED

TODAY'S MOOD

HOMEWORK

BEST CLASS
_____

LUNCH

TOP 3 THINGS THAT HAPPENED

1

2

3

DAILY DOODLE

DAY 29

DATE: _____

TODAY'S MOOD

☺ 😐 ☹

TODAY I LEARNED

HOMEWORK

BEST CLASS
_____

LUNCH

TOP 3 THINGS THAT HAPPENED

1

2

3

DAILY DOODLE

DAY 30

DATE: _____

TODAY I LEARNED

TODAY'S MOOD

HOMEWORK

BEST CLASS

LUNCH

TOP 3 THINGS THAT HAPPENED

1

2

3

DAILY DOODLE

DAY 31

DATE: _____

TODAY I LEARNED

TODAY'S MOOD

HOMEWORK

BEST CLASS

_____

LUNCH

TOP 3 THINGS THAT HAPPENED

1

2

3

DAILY DOODLE

DAY 32

DATE: _____

TODAY I LEARNED

TODAY'S MOOD

HOMEWORK

BEST CLASS
_____

LUNCH

TOP 3 THINGS THAT HAPPENED

1

2

3

DAILY DOODLE

DAY 33

DATE: _____

TODAY'S MOOD

TODAY I LEARNED

HOMEWORK

BEST CLASS

_____

LUNCH

TOP 3 THINGS THAT HAPPENED

1

2

3

DAILY DOODLE

DAY 34

DATE: _____

TODAY I LEARNED

TODAY'S MOOD

HOMEWORK

BEST CLASS
_____

LUNCH

TOP 3 THINGS THAT HAPPENED

1

2

3

DAILY DOODLE

DAY 35

DATE: _____

TODAY'S MOOD

TODAY I LEARNED

HOMEWORK

BEST CLASS _____

LUNCH

TOP 3 THINGS THAT HAPPENED

1

2

3

DAILY DOODLE

DAY 36

DATE: _____

TODAY I LEARNED

TODAY'S MOOD

HOMEWORK

BEST CLASS

_____

LUNCH

TOP 3 THINGS THAT HAPPENED

1

2

3

DAILY DOODLE

DAY 37

DATE: _____

TODAY I LEARNED

TODAY'S MOOD

HOMEWORK

BEST CLASS

LUNCH

TOP 3 THINGS THAT HAPPENED

1

2

3

DAILY DOODLE

DAY 38

DATE: _____

TODAY'S MOOD

TODAY I LEARNED

HOMEWORK

BEST CLASS
_____

LUNCH

TOP 3 THINGS THAT HAPPENED

1

2

3

DAILY DOODLE

DAY 39

DATE: _____

TODAY I LEARNED

TODAY'S MOOD

HOMEWORK

BEST CLASS

LUNCH

TOP 3 THINGS THAT HAPPENED

1

2

3

DAILY DOODLE

DAY 40

DATE: _____

TODAY I LEARNED

TODAY'S MOOD

HOMEWORK

BEST CLASS
_____

LUNCH

TOP 3 THINGS THAT HAPPENED

1

2

3

DAILY DOODLE

DAY 41

DATE: _____

TODAY I LEARNED

TODAY'S MOOD

HOMEWORK

BEST CLASS

_____

LUNCH

TOP 3 THINGS THAT HAPPENED

1

2

3

DAILY DOODLE

DAY 42

DATE: _____

TODAY I LEARNED

TODAY'S MOOD

HOMEWORK

BEST CLASS

LUNCH

TOP 3 THINGS THAT HAPPENED

1

2

3

DAILY DOODLE

DAY 43

DATE: _____

TODAY I LEARNED

TODAY'S MOOD

HOMEWORK

BEST CLASS
_____

LUNCH

TOP 3 THINGS THAT HAPPENED

1

2

3

DAILY DOODLE

DAY 44

DATE: _____

TODAY'S MOOD

TODAY I LEARNED

HOMEWORK

BEST CLASS
_____

LUNCH

TOP 3 THINGS THAT HAPPENED

1

2

3

DAILY DOODLE

DAY 45

DATE: _____

TODAY'S MOOD

TODAY I LEARNED

HOMEWORK

BEST CLASS

_____

LUNCH

TOP 3 THINGS THAT HAPPENED

1

2

3

DAILY DOODLE

DAY 46

DATE: _____

TODAY I LEARNED

TODAY'S MOOD

HOMEWORK

BEST CLASS

_____

LUNCH

TOP 3 THINGS THAT HAPPENED

1

2

3

DAILY DOODLE

DAY 47

DATE: _____

TODAY I LEARNED

TODAY'S MOOD

HOMEWORK

BEST CLASS

LUNCH

TOP 3 THINGS THAT HAPPENED

1

2

3

DAILY DOODLE

DAY 48

DATE: _____

TODAY'S MOOD

TODAY I LEARNED

HOMEWORK

BEST CLASS
_____

LUNCH

TOP 3 THINGS THAT HAPPENED

1

2

3

DAILY DOODLE

DAY 49

DATE: _____

TODAY I LEARNED

TODAY'S MOOD

HOMEWORK

BEST CLASS
_____

LUNCH

TOP 3 THINGS THAT HAPPENED

1

2

3

DAILY DOODLE

DAY 50

DATE: _____

TODAY I LEARNED

TODAY'S MOOD

HOMEWORK

BEST CLASS
_____

LUNCH

TOP 3 THINGS THAT HAPPENED

1

2

3

DAILY DOODLE

DAY 51

DATE: _____

TODAY I LEARNED

TODAY'S MOOD

HOMEWORK

BEST CLASS
_____

LUNCH

TOP 3 THINGS THAT HAPPENED

1

2

3

DAILY DOODLE

DAY 52

DATE: _____

TODAY I LEARNED

TODAY'S MOOD

HOMEWORK

BEST CLASS

LUNCH

TOP 3 THINGS THAT HAPPENED

1

2

3

DAILY DOODLE

DAY 53

DATE: _____

TODAY'S MOOD

TODAY I LEARNED

HOMEWORK

BEST CLASS
_____

LUNCH

TOP 3 THINGS THAT HAPPENED

1

2

3

DAILY DOODLE

DAY 54

DATE: _____

TODAY I LEARNED

TODAY'S MOOD

HOMEWORK

BEST CLASS

LUNCH

TOP 3 THINGS THAT HAPPENED

1

2

3

DAILY DOODLE

DAY 55

DATE: _____

TODAY I LEARNED

TODAY'S MOOD

HOMEWORK

BEST CLASS

_____

LUNCH

TOP 3 THINGS THAT HAPPENED

1

2

3

DAILY DOODLE

DAY 56

DATE: _____

TODAY I LEARNED

TODAY'S MOOD

HOMEWORK

BEST CLASS
_____

LUNCH

TOP 3 THINGS THAT HAPPENED

1

2

3

DAILY DOODLE

DAY 57

DATE: _____

TODAY I LEARNED

TODAY'S MOOD

HOMEWORK

BEST CLASS
_____

LUNCH

TOP 3 THINGS THAT HAPPENED

1

2

3

DAILY DOODLE

DAY 58

DATE: _____

TODAY I LEARNED

TODAY'S MOOD

HOMEWORK

BEST CLASS

LUNCH

TOP 3 THINGS THAT HAPPENED

1

2

3

DAILY DOODLE

DAY 59

DATE: _____

TODAY I LEARNED

TODAY'S MOOD

HOMEWORK

BEST CLASS
_____

LUNCH

TOP 3 THINGS THAT HAPPENED

1

2

3

DAILY DOODLE

DAY 60

DATE: _____

TODAY I LEARNED

TODAY'S MOOD

HOMEWORK

BEST CLASS
_____

LUNCH

TOP 3 THINGS THAT HAPPENED

1

2

3

DAILY DOODLE

DAY 61

DATE: _____

TODAY I LEARNED

TODAY'S MOOD

HOMEWORK

BEST CLASS
_____

LUNCH

TOP 3 THINGS THAT HAPPENED

1

2

3

DAILY DOODLE

DAY 62

DATE: _____

TODAY'S MOOD

TODAY I LEARNED

HOMEWORK

BEST CLASS
_____

LUNCH

TOP 3 THINGS THAT HAPPENED

1

2

3

DAILY DOODLE

DAY 63

DATE: _____

TODAY I LEARNED

TODAY'S MOOD

HOMEWORK

BEST CLASS
_____

LUNCH

TOP 3 THINGS THAT HAPPENED

1

2

3

DAILY DOODLE

DAY 64

DATE: _____

TODAY I LEARNED

TODAY'S MOOD

HOMEWORK

BEST CLASS

_____

LUNCH

TOP 3 THINGS THAT HAPPENED

1

2

3

DAILY DOODLE

DAY 65

DATE: _____

TODAY'S MOOD

TODAY I LEARNED

HOMEWORK

BEST CLASS

LUNCH

TOP 3 THINGS THAT HAPPENED

1

2

3

DAILY DOODLE

DAY 66

DATE: _____

TODAY I LEARNED

TODAY'S MOOD

HOMEWORK

BEST CLASS

LUNCH

TOP 3 THINGS THAT HAPPENED

1

2

3

DAILY DOODLE

DAY 67

DATE: _____

TODAY'S MOOD

TODAY I LEARNED

HOMEWORK

BEST CLASS
_____

LUNCH

TOP 3 THINGS THAT HAPPENED

1

2

3

DAILY DOODLE

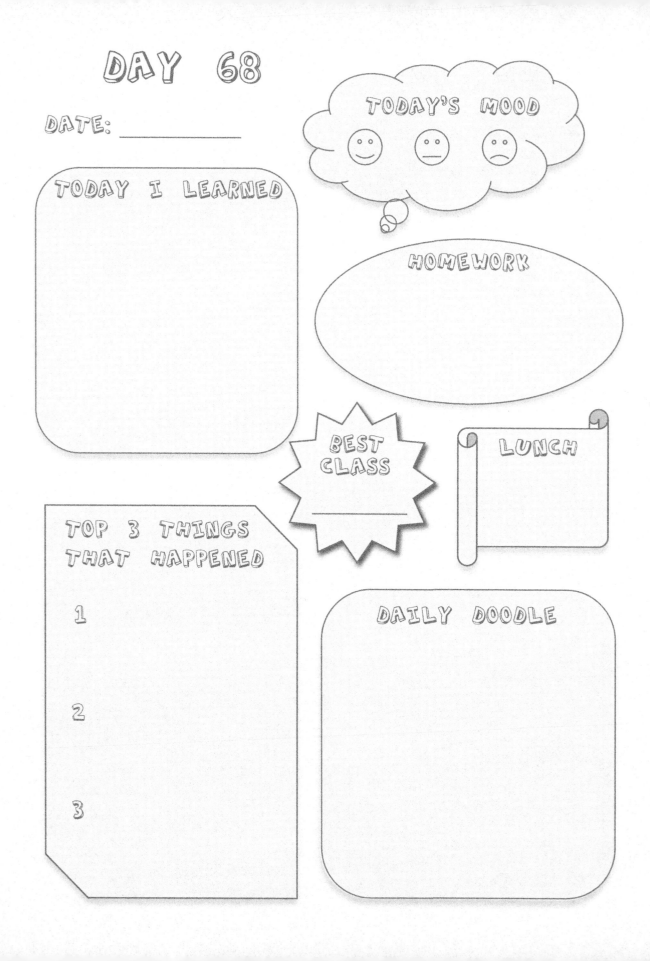

DAY 69

DATE: _____

TODAY I LEARNED

TODAY'S MOOD

HOMEWORK

BEST CLASS

LUNCH

TOP 3 THINGS THAT HAPPENED

1

2

3

DAILY DOODLE

DAY 70

DATE: _____

TODAY I LEARNED

TODAY'S MOOD

HOMEWORK

BEST CLASS
_____

LUNCH

TOP 3 THINGS THAT HAPPENED

1

2

3

DAILY DOODLE

DAY 71

DATE: _____

TODAY I LEARNED

TODAY'S MOOD

HOMEWORK

BEST CLASS
_____

LUNCH

TOP 3 THINGS THAT HAPPENED

1

2

3

DAILY DOODLE

DAY 72

DATE: _____

TODAY I LEARNED

TODAY'S MOOD

HOMEWORK

BEST CLASS

_____

LUNCH

TOP 3 THINGS THAT HAPPENED

1

2

3

DAILY DOODLE

DAY 73

DATE: _____

TODAY I LEARNED

TODAY'S MOOD

HOMEWORK

BEST CLASS
_____

LUNCH

TOP 3 THINGS THAT HAPPENED

1

2

3

DAILY DOODLE

DAY 74

DATE: _____

TODAY I LEARNED

TODAY'S MOOD

HOMEWORK

BEST CLASS

_____

LUNCH

TOP 3 THINGS THAT HAPPENED

1

2

3

DAILY DOODLE

DAY 75

DATE: _____

TODAY'S MOOD

TODAY I LEARNED

HOMEWORK

BEST CLASS
_____

LUNCH

TOP 3 THINGS THAT HAPPENED

1

2

3

DAILY DOODLE

DAY 76

DATE: _____

TODAY I LEARNED

TODAY'S MOOD

HOMEWORK

BEST CLASS

LUNCH

TOP 3 THINGS THAT HAPPENED

1

2

3

DAILY DOODLE

DAY 77

DATE: _____

TODAY I LEARNED

TODAY'S MOOD

HOMEWORK

BEST CLASS
_____

LUNCH

TOP 3 THINGS THAT HAPPENED

1

2

3

DAILY DOODLE

DAY 78

DATE: _____

TODAY I LEARNED

TODAY'S MOOD

HOMEWORK

BEST CLASS

_____

LUNCH

TOP 3 THINGS THAT HAPPENED

1

2

3

DAILY DOODLE

DAY 79

DATE: _____

TODAY'S MOOD

TODAY I LEARNED

HOMEWORK

BEST CLASS

_____

LUNCH

TOP 3 THINGS THAT HAPPENED

1

2

3

DAILY DOODLE

DAY 80

DATE: _____

TODAY I LEARNED

TODAY'S MOOD

HOMEWORK

BEST CLASS
_____

LUNCH

TOP 3 THINGS THAT HAPPENED

1

2

3

DAILY DOODLE

DAY 81

DATE: _____

TODAY'S MOOD

TODAY I LEARNED

HOMEWORK

BEST CLASS
_____

LUNCH

TOP 3 THINGS THAT HAPPENED

1

2

3

DAILY DOODLE

DAY 82

DATE: _____

TODAY I LEARNED

TODAY'S MOOD

HOMEWORK

BEST CLASS
_____

LUNCH

TOP 3 THINGS THAT HAPPENED

1

2

3

DAILY DOODLE

DAY 83

DATE: _____

TODAY I LEARNED

TODAY'S MOOD

HOMEWORK

BEST CLASS

_____

LUNCH

TOP 3 THINGS THAT HAPPENED

1

2

3

DAILY DOODLE

DAY 84

DATE: _____

TODAY I LEARNED

TODAY'S MOOD

HOMEWORK

BEST CLASS
_____

LUNCH

TOP 3 THINGS THAT HAPPENED

1

2

3

DAILY DOODLE

DAY 85

DATE: _____

TODAY'S MOOD

TODAY I LEARNED

HOMEWORK

BEST CLASS
_____

LUNCH

TOP 3 THINGS THAT HAPPENED

1

2

3

DAILY DOODLE

DAY 86

DATE: _____

TODAY I LEARNED

TODAY'S MOOD

HOMEWORK

BEST CLASS

LUNCH

TOP 3 THINGS THAT HAPPENED

1

2

3

DAILY DOODLE

DAY 87

DATE: _____

TODAY I LEARNED

TODAY'S MOOD

HOMEWORK

BEST CLASS

LUNCH

TOP 3 THINGS THAT HAPPENED

1

2

3

DAILY DOODLE

DAY 88

DATE: _____

TODAY I LEARNED

TODAY'S MOOD

HOMEWORK

BEST CLASS

_____

LUNCH

TOP 3 THINGS THAT HAPPENED

1

2

3

DAILY DOODLE

DAY 89

DATE: _____

TODAY I LEARNED

TODAY'S MOOD

HOMEWORK

BEST CLASS
_____

LUNCH

TOP 3 THINGS THAT HAPPENED

1

2

3

DAILY DOODLE

DAY 90

DATE: _____

TODAY I LEARNED

TODAY'S MOOD

HOMEWORK

BEST CLASS
_____

LUNCH

TOP 3 THINGS THAT HAPPENED

1

2

3

DAILY DOODLE

DAY 91

DATE: _____

TODAY'S MOOD

TODAY I LEARNED

HOMEWORK

BEST CLASS

_____

LUNCH

TOP 3 THINGS THAT HAPPENED

1

2

3

DAILY DOODLE

DAY 92

DATE: _____

TODAY'S MOOD

TODAY I LEARNED

HOMEWORK

BEST CLASS

LUNCH

TOP 3 THINGS THAT HAPPENED

1

2

3

DAILY DOODLE

DAY 93

DATE: _____

TODAY I LEARNED

TODAY'S MOOD

HOMEWORK

BEST CLASS
_____

LUNCH

TOP 3 THINGS THAT HAPPENED

1

2

3

DAILY DOODLE

DAY 95

DATE: _____

TODAY I LEARNED

TODAY'S MOOD

HOMEWORK

BEST CLASS
_____

TOP 3 THINGS THAT HAPPENED

1

2

3

LUNCH

DAILY DOODLE

DAY 96

DATE: _____

TODAY I LEARNED

TODAY'S MOOD

HOMEWORK

BEST CLASS

LUNCH

TOP 3 THINGS THAT HAPPENED

1

2

3

DAILY DOODLE

DAY 97

DATE: _____

TODAY I LEARNED

TODAY'S MOOD

HOMEWORK

BEST CLASS

_____

LUNCH

TOP 3 THINGS THAT HAPPENED

1

2

3

DAILY DOODLE

DAY 98

DATE: _____

TODAY I LEARNED

TODAY'S MOOD

HOMEWORK

BEST CLASS
_____

LUNCH

TOP 3 THINGS THAT HAPPENED

1

2

3

DAILY DOODLE

DAY 99

DATE: _____

TODAY I LEARNED

TODAY'S MOOD

HOMEWORK

BEST CLASS

_____

LUNCH

TOP 3 THINGS THAT HAPPENED

1

2

3

DAILY DOODLE

DAY 100

DATE: _____

TODAY I LEARNED

TODAY'S MOOD

HOMEWORK

BEST CLASS
_____

LUNCH

TOP 3 THINGS THAT HAPPENED

1

2

3

DAILY DOODLE

DAY 101

DATE: _____

TODAY'S MOOD

TODAY I LEARNED

HOMEWORK

BEST CLASS

_____

LUNCH

TOP 3 THINGS THAT HAPPENED

1

2

3

DAILY DOODLE

DAY 102

DATE: _____

TODAY I LEARNED

TODAY'S MOOD

HOMEWORK

BEST CLASS
_____

LUNCH

TOP 3 THINGS THAT HAPPENED

1

2

3

DAILY DOODLE

DAY 104

DATE: _____

TODAY I LEARNED

TODAY'S MOOD

HOMEWORK

BEST CLASS
_____

LUNCH

TOP 3 THINGS THAT HAPPENED

1

2

3

DAILY DOODLE

DAY 105

DATE: _____

TODAY I LEARNED

TODAY'S MOOD

HOMEWORK

BEST CLASS
_____

LUNCH

TOP 3 THINGS THAT HAPPENED

1

2

3

DAILY DOODLE

DAY 106

DATE: _____

TODAY I LEARNED

TODAY'S MOOD

HOMEWORK

BEST CLASS

_____

LUNCH

TOP 3 THINGS THAT HAPPENED

1

2

3

DAILY DOODLE

DAY 107

DATE: _____

TODAY'S MOOD

TODAY I LEARNED

HOMEWORK

BEST CLASS
_____

LUNCH

TOP 3 THINGS THAT HAPPENED

1

2

3

DAILY DOODLE

DAY 108

DATE: _____

TODAY I LEARNED

TODAY'S MOOD

HOMEWORK

BEST CLASS
_____

LUNCH

TOP 3 THINGS THAT HAPPENED

1

2

3

DAILY DOODLE

DAY 109

DATE: _____

TODAY'S MOOD

TODAY I LEARNED

HOMEWORK

BEST CLASS

_____

LUNCH

TOP 3 THINGS THAT HAPPENED

1

2

3

DAILY DOODLE

DAY 110

DATE: _____

TODAY I LEARNED

TODAY'S MOOD

HOMEWORK

BEST CLASS

LUNCH

TOP 3 THINGS THAT HAPPENED

1

2

3

DAILY DOODLE

DAY 111

DATE: _____

TODAY I LEARNED

TODAY'S MOOD

HOMEWORK

TOP 3 THINGS THAT HAPPENED

1

2

3

BEST CLASS

_____

LUNCH

DAILY DOODLE

DAY 112

DATE: _____

TODAY I LEARNED

TODAY'S MOOD

HOMEWORK

BEST CLASS
_____

LUNCH

TOP 3 THINGS THAT HAPPENED

1

2

3

DAILY DOODLE

DAY 113

DATE: _____

TODAY I LEARNED

TODAY'S MOOD

HOMEWORK

BEST CLASS

_____

LUNCH

TOP 3 THINGS THAT HAPPENED

1

2

3

DAILY DOODLE

DAY 114

DATE: _____

TODAY'S MOOD

TODAY I LEARNED

HOMEWORK

BEST CLASS
_____

LUNCH

TOP 3 THINGS THAT HAPPENED

1

2

3

DAILY DOODLE

DAY 115

DATE: _____

TODAY I LEARNED

TODAY'S MOOD

HOMEWORK

BEST CLASS

_____

LUNCH

TOP 3 THINGS THAT HAPPENED

1

2

3

DAILY DOODLE

DAY 116

DATE: _____

TODAY I LEARNED

TODAY'S MOOD

HOMEWORK

BEST CLASS

LUNCH

TOP 3 THINGS THAT HAPPENED

1

2

3

DAILY DOODLE

DAY 117

DATE: _____

TODAY'S MOOD

TODAY I LEARNED

HOMEWORK

BEST CLASS

LUNCH

TOP 3 THINGS THAT HAPPENED

1

2

3

DAILY DOODLE

DAY 118

DATE: _____

TODAY I LEARNED

TODAY'S MOOD

HOMEWORK

BEST CLASS
_____

LUNCH

TOP 3 THINGS THAT HAPPENED

1

2

3

DAILY DOODLE

DAY 119

DATE: _____

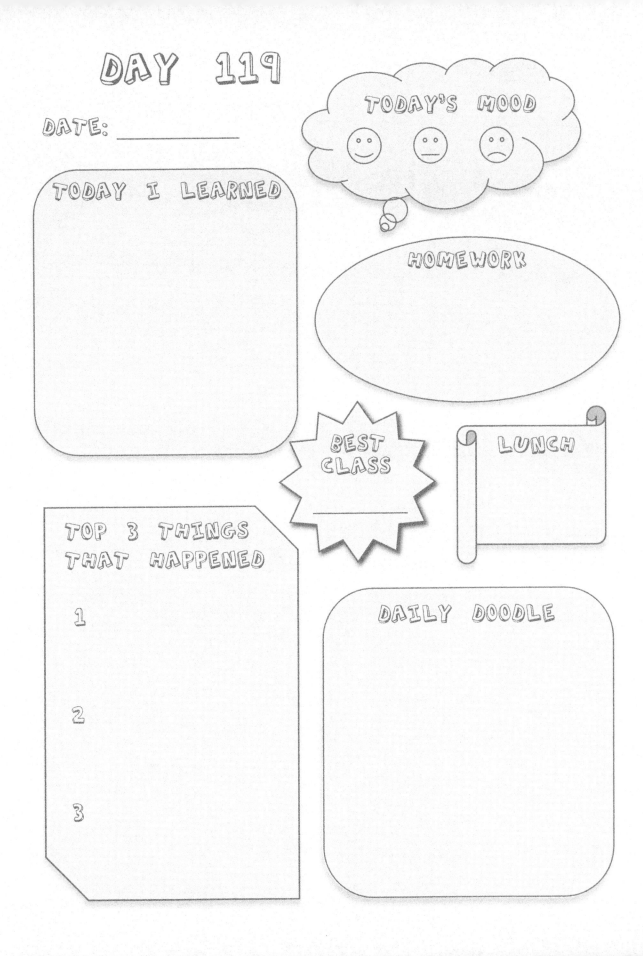

TODAY I LEARNED

TODAY'S MOOD

HOMEWORK

BEST CLASS

LUNCH

TOP 3 THINGS THAT HAPPENED

1

2

3

DAILY DOODLE

DAY 120

DATE: _____

TODAY I LEARNED

TODAY'S MOOD

HOMEWORK

BEST CLASS

_____

LUNCH

TOP 3 THINGS THAT HAPPENED

1

2

3

DAILY DOODLE

DAY 121

DATE: _____

TODAY I LEARNED

TODAY'S MOOD

HOMEWORK

BEST CLASS
_____

LUNCH

TOP 3 THINGS THAT HAPPENED

1

2

3

DAILY DOODLE

DAY 122

DATE: _____

TODAY I LEARNED

TODAY'S MOOD

HOMEWORK

BEST CLASS
_____

LUNCH

TOP 3 THINGS THAT HAPPENED

1

2

3

DAILY DOODLE

DAY 123

DATE: _____

TODAY'S MOOD

TODAY I LEARNED

HOMEWORK

BEST CLASS
_____

LUNCH

TOP 3 THINGS THAT HAPPENED

1

2

3

DAILY DOODLE

DAY 124

DATE: _____

TODAY I LEARNED

TODAY'S MOOD

HOMEWORK

BEST CLASS
_____

LUNCH

TOP 3 THINGS THAT HAPPENED

1

2

3

DAILY DOODLE

DAY 125

DATE: _____

TODAY'S MOOD

TODAY I LEARNED

HOMEWORK

BEST CLASS
_____

LUNCH

TOP 3 THINGS THAT HAPPENED

1

2

3

DAILY DOODLE

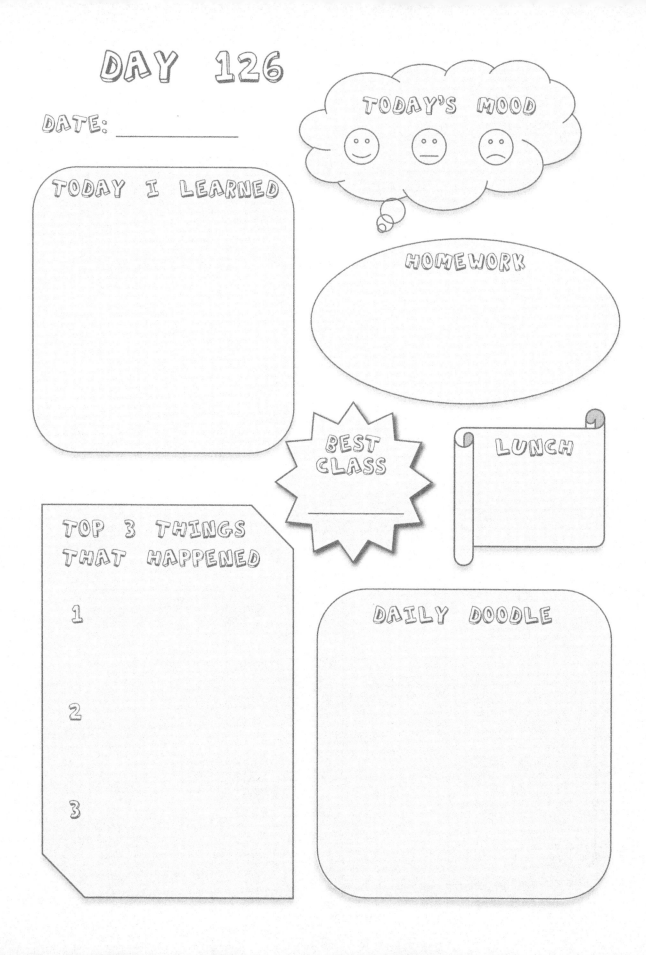

DAY 127

DATE: _____

TODAY I LEARNED

TODAY'S MOOD

HOMEWORK

BEST CLASS
_____

LUNCH

TOP 3 THINGS THAT HAPPENED

1

2

3

DAILY DOODLE

DAY 128

DATE: _____

TODAY I LEARNED

TODAY'S MOOD

HOMEWORK

BEST CLASS

_____

LUNCH

TOP 3 THINGS THAT HAPPENED

1

2

3

DAILY DOODLE

DAY 129

DATE: _____

TODAY'S MOOD

TODAY I LEARNED

HOMEWORK

BEST CLASS

_____

LUNCH

TOP 3 THINGS THAT HAPPENED

1

2

3

DAILY DOODLE

DAY 130

DATE: _____

TODAY I LEARNED

TODAY'S MOOD

HOMEWORK

BEST CLASS
_____

LUNCH

TOP 3 THINGS THAT HAPPENED

1

2

3

DAILY DOODLE

DAY 131

DATE: _____

TODAY I LEARNED

TODAY'S MOOD

HOMEWORK

BEST CLASS
_____

LUNCH

TOP 3 THINGS THAT HAPPENED

1

2

3

DAILY DOODLE

DAY 132

DATE: _____

TODAY I LEARNED

TODAY'S MOOD

HOMEWORK

BEST CLASS
_____

LUNCH

TOP 3 THINGS THAT HAPPENED

1

2

3

DAILY DOODLE

DAY 134

DATE: _____

TODAY I LEARNED

TODAY'S MOOD

HOMEWORK

BEST CLASS

LUNCH

TOP 3 THINGS THAT HAPPENED

1

2

3

DAILY DOODLE

DAY 135

DATE: _____

TODAY'S MOOD

TODAY I LEARNED

HOMEWORK

BEST CLASS
_____

LUNCH

TOP 3 THINGS THAT HAPPENED

1

2

3

DAILY DOODLE

DAY 136

DATE: _____

TODAY I LEARNED

TODAY'S MOOD

HOMEWORK

BEST CLASS
_____

LUNCH

TOP 3 THINGS THAT HAPPENED

1

2

3

DAILY DOODLE

DAY 137

DATE: _____

TODAY'S MOOD

TODAY I LEARNED

HOMEWORK

BEST CLASS
_____

LUNCH

TOP 3 THINGS THAT HAPPENED

1

2

3

DAILY DOODLE

DAY 138

DATE: _____

TODAY I LEARNED

TODAY'S MOOD

HOMEWORK

BEST CLASS
_____

LUNCH

TOP 3 THINGS THAT HAPPENED

1

2

3

DAILY DOODLE

DAY 139

DATE: _____

TODAY I LEARNED

TODAY'S MOOD

HOMEWORK

BEST CLASS

LUNCH

TOP 3 THINGS THAT HAPPENED

1

2

3

DAILY DOODLE

DAY 140

DATE: _____

TODAY I LEARNED

TODAY'S MOOD

HOMEWORK

BEST CLASS
_____

LUNCH

TOP 3 THINGS THAT HAPPENED

1

2

3

DAILY DOODLE

DAY 141

DATE: _____

TODAY I LEARNED

TODAY'S MOOD

HOMEWORK

BEST CLASS
_____

LUNCH

TOP 3 THINGS THAT HAPPENED

1

2

3

DAILY DOODLE

DAY 142

DATE: _____

TODAY I LEARNED

TODAY'S MOOD

HOMEWORK

TOP 3 THINGS THAT HAPPENED

1

2

3

BEST CLASS
_____

LUNCH

DAILY DOODLE

DAY 143

DATE: _____

TODAY'S MOOD

TODAY I LEARNED

HOMEWORK

BEST CLASS
_____

LUNCH

TOP 3 THINGS THAT HAPPENED

1

2

3

DAILY DOODLE

DAY 144

DATE: _____

TODAY I LEARNED

TODAY'S MOOD

HOMEWORK

BEST CLASS

LUNCH

TOP 3 THINGS THAT HAPPENED

1

2

3

DAILY DOODLE

DAY 145

DATE: _____

TODAY I LEARNED

TODAY'S MOOD

HOMEWORK

BEST CLASS
_____

LUNCH

TOP 3 THINGS THAT HAPPENED

1

2

3

DAILY DOODLE

DAY 146

DATE: _____

TODAY I LEARNED

TODAY'S MOOD

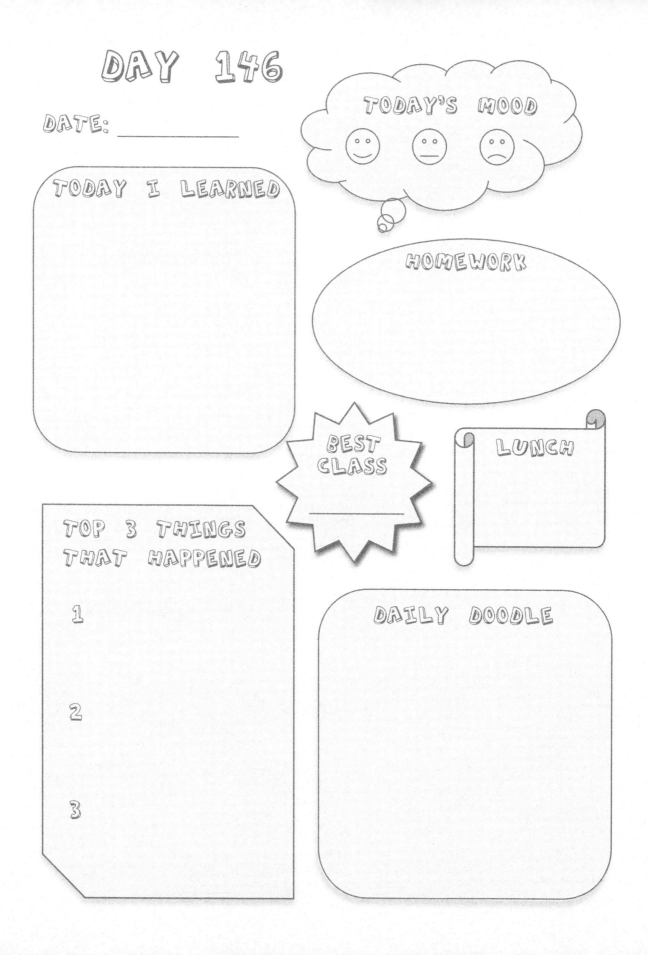

HOMEWORK

BEST CLASS
_____

LUNCH

TOP 3 THINGS THAT HAPPENED

1

2

3

DAILY DOODLE

DAY 148

DATE: _____

TODAY I LEARNED

TODAY'S MOOD

HOMEWORK

BEST CLASS
_____

LUNCH

TOP 3 THINGS THAT HAPPENED

1

2

3

DAILY DOODLE

DAY 149

DATE: _____

TODAY'S MOOD

TODAY I LEARNED

HOMEWORK

BEST CLASS

LUNCH

TOP 3 THINGS THAT HAPPENED

1

2

3

DAILY DOODLE

DAY 150

DATE: _____

TODAY I LEARNED

TODAY'S MOOD

HOMEWORK

BEST CLASS
_____

LUNCH

TOP 3 THINGS THAT HAPPENED

1

2

3

DAILY DOODLE

DAY 151

DATE: _____

TODAY'S MOOD

TODAY I LEARNED

HOMEWORK

BEST CLASS

LUNCH

TOP 3 THINGS THAT HAPPENED

1

2

3

DAILY DOODLE

DAY 152

DATE: _____

TODAY I LEARNED

TODAY'S MOOD

HOMEWORK

BEST CLASS
_____

LUNCH

TOP 3 THINGS THAT HAPPENED

1

2

3

DAILY DOODLE

DAY 153

DATE: _____

TODAY'S MOOD

TODAY I LEARNED

HOMEWORK

BEST CLASS
_____

LUNCH

TOP 3 THINGS THAT HAPPENED

1

2

3

DAILY DOODLE

DAY 154

DATE: _____

TODAY I LEARNED

TODAY'S MOOD

HOMEWORK

BEST CLASS

_____

LUNCH

TOP 3 THINGS THAT HAPPENED

1

2

3

DAILY DOODLE

DAY 155

DATE: _____

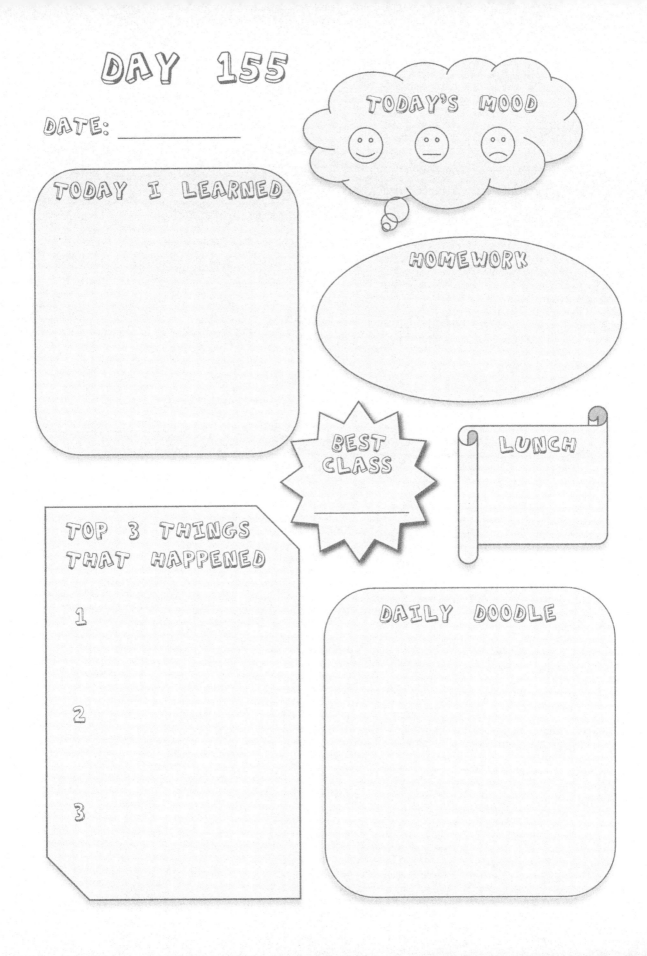

TODAY I LEARNED

TODAY'S MOOD

HOMEWORK

BEST CLASS

LUNCH

TOP 3 THINGS THAT HAPPENED

1

2

3

DAILY DOODLE

DAY 156

DATE: _____

TODAY I LEARNED

TODAY'S MOOD

HOMEWORK

TOP 3 THINGS THAT HAPPENED

1

2

3

BEST CLASS

_____

LUNCH

DAILY DOODLE

DAY 157

DATE: _____

TODAY I LEARNED

TODAY'S MOOD

HOMEWORK

BEST CLASS

LUNCH

TOP 3 THINGS THAT HAPPENED

1

2

3

DAILY DOODLE

DAY 158

DATE: _____

TODAY I LEARNED

TODAY'S MOOD

HOMEWORK

BEST CLASS
_____

LUNCH

TOP 3 THINGS THAT HAPPENED

1

2

3

DAILY DOODLE

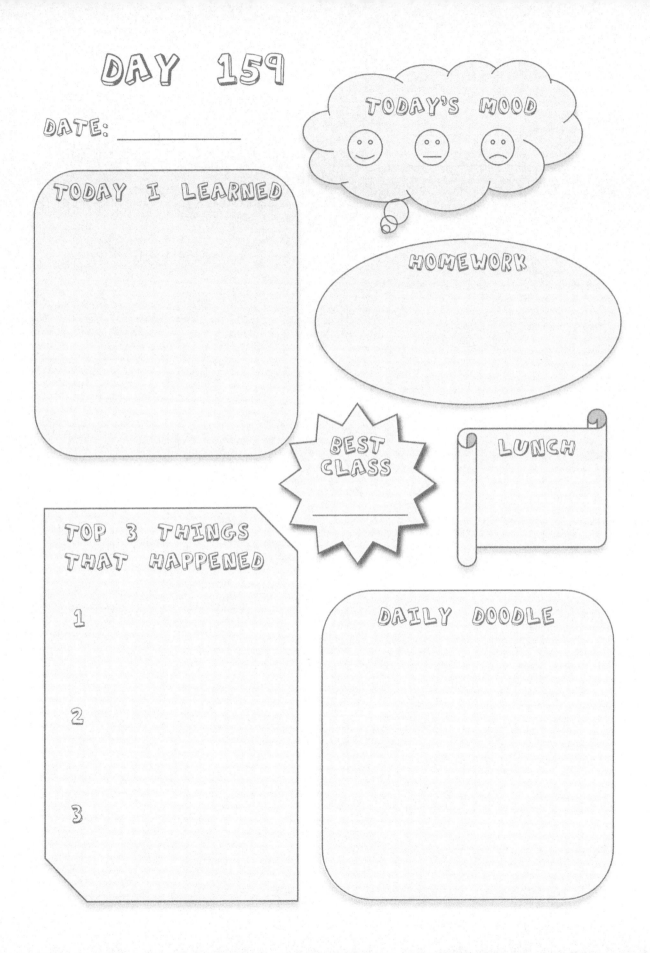

DAY 159

DATE: _____

TODAY'S MOOD

TODAY I LEARNED

HOMEWORK

BEST CLASS

LUNCH

TOP 3 THINGS THAT HAPPENED

1

2

3

DAILY DOODLE

DAY 160

DATE: _____

TODAY I LEARNED

TODAY'S MOOD

HOMEWORK

BEST CLASS

LUNCH

TOP 3 THINGS THAT HAPPENED

1

2

3

DAILY DOODLE

DAY 161

DATE: _____

TODAY I LEARNED

TODAY'S MOOD

HOMEWORK

BEST CLASS

LUNCH

TOP 3 THINGS THAT HAPPENED

1

2

3

DAILY DOODLE

DAY 162

DATE: _____

TODAY I LEARNED

TODAY'S MOOD

HOMEWORK

BEST CLASS

LUNCH

TOP 3 THINGS THAT HAPPENED

1

2

3

DAILY DOODLE

DAY 163

DATE: _____

TODAY I LEARNED

TODAY'S MOOD

HOMEWORK

BEST CLASS

_____

LUNCH

TOP 3 THINGS THAT HAPPENED

1

2

3

DAILY DOODLE

DAY 164

DATE: _____

TODAY I LEARNED

TODAY'S MOOD

HOMEWORK

BEST CLASS
_____

LUNCH

TOP 3 THINGS THAT HAPPENED

1

2

3

DAILY DOODLE

DAY 165

DATE: _____

TODAY I LEARNED

TODAY'S MOOD

HOMEWORK

TOP 3 THINGS THAT HAPPENED

1

2

3

BEST CLASS

_____

LUNCH

DAILY DOODLE

DAY 166

DATE: _____

TODAY I LEARNED

TODAY'S MOOD

HOMEWORK

BEST CLASS

LUNCH

TOP 3 THINGS THAT HAPPENED

1

2

3

DAILY DOODLE

DAY 167

DATE: _____

TODAY I LEARNED

TODAY'S MOOD

HOMEWORK

BEST CLASS

_____

LUNCH

TOP 3 THINGS THAT HAPPENED

1

2

3

DAILY DOODLE

DAY 168

DATE: _____

TODAY I LEARNED

TODAY'S MOOD

HOMEWORK

BEST CLASS

LUNCH

TOP 3 THINGS THAT HAPPENED

1

2

3

DAILY DOODLE

DAY 169

DATE: _____

TODAY I LEARNED

TODAY'S MOOD

HOMEWORK

BEST CLASS
_____

LUNCH

TOP 3 THINGS THAT HAPPENED

1

2

3

DAILY DOODLE

DAY 170

DATE: _____

TODAY I LEARNED

TODAY'S MOOD

HOMEWORK

BEST CLASS

LUNCH

TOP 3 THINGS THAT HAPPENED

1

2

3

DAILY DOODLE

DAY 171

DATE: _____

TODAY'S MOOD

TODAY I LEARNED

HOMEWORK

BEST CLASS
_____

LUNCH

TOP 3 THINGS THAT HAPPENED

1

2

3

DAILY DOODLE

DAY 172

DATE: _____

TODAY I LEARNED

TODAY'S MOOD

HOMEWORK

BEST CLASS
_____

LUNCH

TOP 3 THINGS THAT HAPPENED

1

2

3

DAILY DOODLE

DAY 175

DATE: _____

TODAY'S MOOD

TODAY I LEARNED

HOMEWORK

BEST CLASS
_____

LUNCH

TOP 3 THINGS THAT HAPPENED

1

2

3

DAILY DOODLE

DAY 176

DATE: _____

TODAY I LEARNED

TODAY'S MOOD

HOMEWORK

BEST CLASS

_____

LUNCH

TOP 3 THINGS THAT HAPPENED

1

2

3

DAILY DOODLE

DAY 177

DATE: _____

TODAY I LEARNED

TODAY'S MOOD

HOMEWORK

TOP 3 THINGS THAT HAPPENED

1

2

3

BEST CLASS

LUNCH

DAILY DOODLE

DAY 178

DATE: _____

TODAY I LEARNED

TODAY'S MOOD

HOMEWORK

BEST CLASS

_____

LUNCH

TOP 3 THINGS THAT HAPPENED

1

2

3

DAILY DOODLE

DAY 179

DATE: _____

TODAY I LEARNED

TODAY'S MOOD

HOMEWORK

BEST CLASS
_____

LUNCH

TOP 3 THINGS THAT HAPPENED

1

2

3

DAILY DOODLE

DAY 180

DATE: _____

TODAY'S MOOD

TODAY I LEARNED

HOMEWORK

BEST CLASS

_____

LUNCH

TOP 3 THINGS THAT HAPPENED

1

2

3

DAILY DOODLE

DAY 181

DATE: _____

TODAY I LEARNED

TODAY'S MOOD

HOMEWORK

BEST CLASS

LUNCH

TOP 3 THINGS THAT HAPPENED

1

2

3

DAILY DOODLE

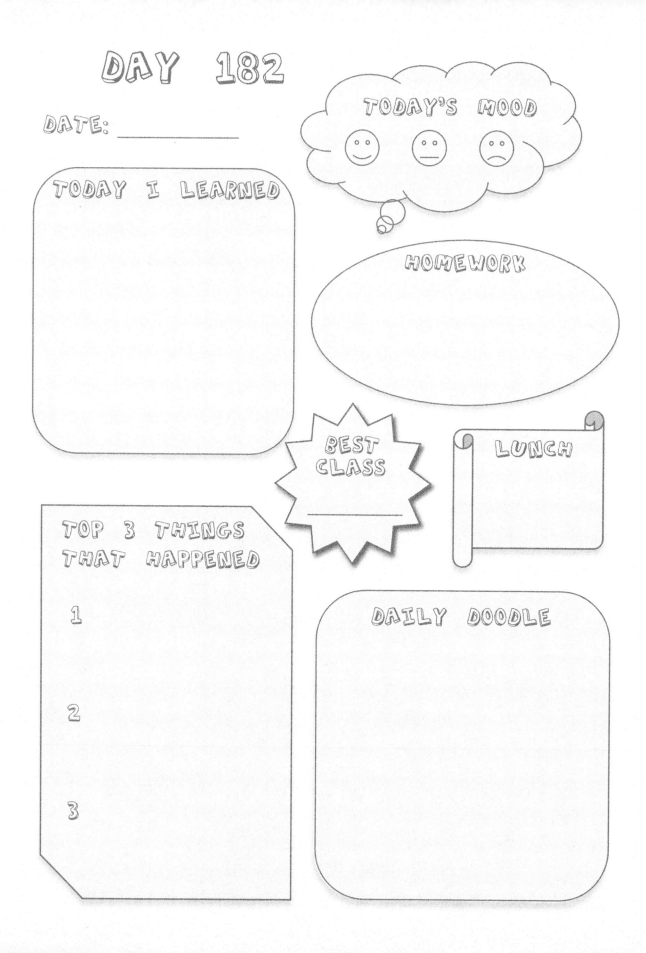

DAY 183

DATE: _____

TODAY I LEARNED

TODAY'S MOOD

HOMEWORK

BEST CLASS

_____

LUNCH

TOP 3 THINGS THAT HAPPENED

1

2

3

DAILY DOODLE

DAY 184

DATE: _____

TODAY I LEARNED

TODAY'S MOOD

HOMEWORK

BEST CLASS
_____

LUNCH

TOP 3 THINGS THAT HAPPENED

1

2

3

DAILY DOODLE

PHOTO OF ME ON LAST DAY OF KINDERGARTEN

BEST THING I LEARNED THIS YEAR:

_____

TODAY I AM FEELING:

THANK YOU FOR YOUR PURCHASE!

Your positive support would be greatly appreciated... please consider leaving a review for this book on Amazon.com!

For more planners, journals, and other specialty books by Jennifer L. Gee, please visit this website:

TIMBERBELLEPRESS.COM